Railways & Recollections 1967
Farewell to SOUTHERN REGION Steam

Contents

Series Introduction

Railway publishing has been around almost as long as the railways themselves and there have been countless books with a historical theme, telling the story of a particular line, say, and occasionally linking the subject to its social context, but never before has there been, in such an accessible way, a juxtapositioning of photographic illustration of a railway subject with the events, happenings and highlights of a wider sphere and calendar. This series take a particular year and places the views displayed alongside a carefully selected pot-pourri of what happened in that twelve-month period. The vast majority of the images in the books are from the Ray Ruffell collection, held by the publisher, but material from other sources is interspersed where felt necessary to maintain appropriate variety. Ray was a railwayman and photographer of equal merit and the main criterion for inclusion in these books is for the images to be both interesting and aesthetically pleasing within a chosen theme.

The books are aimed at a more general market than mere railway aficionados or enthusiasts and the authors hope and trust that they will be sure in their aim and that you, the reader, will find much to enjoy, appreciate, enthuse about and even smile about! And it is hoped that some of your own memories are stirred along the way and that you may wish to share these with friends!

© Chris Harris 2010
Photos: © The NOSTALGIA Collection archive unless otherwise credited.

First published in 2010
ISBN 978 1 85794 336 8
Silver Link Publishing Ltd
The Trundle
Ringstead Road
Great Addington
Kettering
Northants NN14 4BW

Tel/Fax: 01536 330588
email: sales@nostalgiacollection.com
Website: www.nostalgiacollection.com
British Library Cataloguing in Publication Data
A catalogue record for this book is available from the British Library.
Printed and bound in the Czech Republic

Above: **READING** Ray Ruffell stands proudly beside the SR CME's Inspection Saloon DS70155 which is standing in No 6 bay platform at Reading General on 24 October 1966.

Frontispiece: **WATERLOO** It is sad to relate that locomotive number plates and name plates became targets for theft during the last years of steam operation on British Rail's Southern Region. To counter this, the 'powers that be' removed these items from many locomotives, as illustrated by Bulleid Pacific No 34021, seen through the open Bostwick platform gates at London Waterloo. The *Dartmoor* nameplates are conspicuously absent having been removed for safe keeping.

Opposite background: **EASTLEIGH** The substantial bulk of Eastleigh (East) signal box form an impressive backdrop to BR Standard Class '5', 4-6-0 No 73093 on 5 January 1967.

Introduction

Mention the year 1967 to many people of a certain age and they will probably reply 'the summer of love'. However, mention 1967 to any transport enthusiast of similar age who hails from the South of England and the reply will almost certainly be 'the year steam ended on the Southern Region'. Monday 10 July 1967 was indeed a sad day for fans of the steam locomotive, although most of us had stored up many happy memories during the first half of the year as countless hours were spent both watching and riding behind the steam locomotives that remained in service. The atmosphere of that memorable year is well captured in Ray Ruffell's excellent photographs in this book; writing the captions took me instantly back to those teenage days as I recall trips in comfortable Bulleid carriages hauled by locomotives whose condition by that time was sometimes quite decrepit - yet nonetheless almost always seemed to put up a good performance. But all too soon Bulleid Merchant Navy Pacific No 35030 Elder Dempster Lines brought the last steam train into Waterloo the 2.07pm from Weymouth on Sunday 9 July 1967. I had been deeply privileged to live close to the last steam worked main line, but now it was all over.

Actually there was still much of interest in the local railway scene, as some of the new electric units had been delivered later than planned, and various teething problems resulted in a number of fascinating 'scratch' formations sometimes appearing until well into 1968. Also on the road transport side it was still possible to ride around in delightful lowbridge bodied buses if you knew where to look for them; there was still plenty of transport interest to enjoy. Plus the discovery of girls also ameliorated to some degree my mourning over the loss of steam, so the description 'summer of love' also strikes an appropriate chord.

But sadly war was to dominate the international news headlines as much as love during 1967. Many lives were being lost in Vietnam during the year, while the so-called Six Day War between Israel and its Arab neighbours had, in addition to the human misery caused, a less than beneficial effect on the world economy. In Britain, after the financial crisis of July 1966, early forecasts for 1967 had predicted a small surplus in the balance of payments. By the late summer of 1967 those forecasts had been completely reversed to predict a substantial deficit, while unemployment had reached the highest summer total since the 1940s. On 18 November 1967 the pound was devalued from $2.80 to $2.40 together with an accompanying deflationary package that raised bank rate to 8%, imposed hire-purchase restrictions and scaled down public spending.

An even more sombre event that took place during November 1967 was the derailment of a Hastings line Diesel Electric Multiple Unit while working an evening return journey to Charing Cross on Guy Fawkes Day; 49 people were killed and 78 injured in this tragedy that was caused by a broken rail. Earlier in the year a serious and remarkable accident took place on the East Coast Main Line. A pertly derailed freight train was hit by the midday Kings Cross to Edinburgh express; seven passengers were killed and 45 injured. The passenger train had been headed by prototype diesel locomotive DP2, which was so badly damaged that it had to be scrapped.

It was in January 1967 that Housing Minister Anthony Greenwood designated 22,000 acres of Buckinghamshire to be developed as the new town of Milton Keynes. A total of 32 new towns have been developed since the end of the Second World War, but Milton Keynes is certainly the best known, and also the largest purpose built town in England.

Acts of Parliament that helped make Britain a more tolerant and liberal society included the Abortion Act, passed in October 1967, and the decriminalisation of homosexuality in England under the terms of the Sexual Offences Act passed in July. Less well received by many people was the Marine Broadcasting (Offences) Act which closed down the pirate radio stations that during the past few years had broadcast pop music, mostly from ships anchored a few miles off the coast. The pirate stations had been especially enjoyed by teenagers, a fair proportion of whom found little of interest on the BBC at that time. However, on 30 September 1967 a new BBC station, Radio 1, took to the airwaves with this audience in mind - having recruited a number of disc jockeys who had previously worked for the pirate stations! From the same date the existing Light Programme became Radio 2, the Third became Radio 3 and the Home Service became Radio 4. Meanwhile on television BBC 2 programmes were transmitted in colour from 2 December.

Please join me as we revisit this memorable year in Railways and Recollections, 1967 ....

Chris Harris
Poole, Dorset.
February 2010

OUT & ABOUT WITH SOUTHERN REGION STEAM

Below: **EASTLEIGH** A scene we would not be able to enjoy for much longer ...on 5 January 1967 Bulleid West Country Pacific No 34040 *Crewkerne* is passing Eastleigh at the head of a banana train; these were a regular feature of Southern Region operations at the time, and consisted of special steam heated vans to keep this delicious cargo warm. Crewkerne was built in 1946, rebuilt in 1960 and withdrawn in 1967.

Opposite: **WATERLOO** These two photographs show the 12.39pm service from Waterloo to Basingstoke on 7 January 1967. The front carriage is of Bulleid design and carries SR green livery while the remainder of the train is BR Standard Mark I stock in blue and grey. Heading the train is BR Standard Class '4', 2-6-0 No 76011. In the lower view the train eases over the pointwork at the 'throat' of Waterloo station as an incoming suburban electric multiple unit makes for the Windsor line platforms.

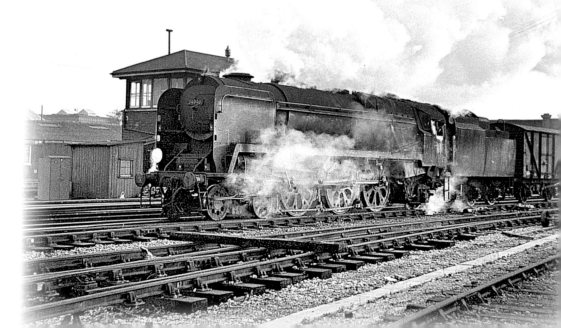

types; some Brush Class '4',7 diesels borrowed from the Western Region hauled a number of trains, plus of course there were the Southern Region's own Type 3 D65XX diesels. And as spring matured into summer the new electric multiple units started to appear. Thus in the last months of steam operation there was plenty to see and enjoy. Moreover, once most of the engineering works associated with electrification had been completed, and the various temporary speed restrictions therefore lifted, many of the locomotive crews entered into the spirit of things and gave some really sparkling and exciting runs.

The many faces of this unique year are well captured in the following pages ....

The sombre winter days we see in these opening photographs illustrate in part the feelings shared at that time by many fans of steam traction, who had greeted the new year with little enthusiasm, knowing that in the forthcoming summer the last steam worked main line in Britain would succumb to electric traction. All was not entirely doom and gloom, however, as the coming months were to see an interesting variety of motive power used on the Waterloo to Bournemouth and Weymouth trains. A depleted stock of Bulleid Pacifics was helped out by various BR Standard steam

1967 Happenings (1)

January

Jeremy Thorpe becomes leader of the Liberal Party.

Milton Keynes designated as a 'new town'

February

British submarine HMS Renown launched

March

Queen Elizabeth Hall opened in London

First North Sea Gas pumped ashore in Yorkshire

Super-tanker Torrey Canyon runs aground off Lands End - later bombed by RAF and sunk

April

UK wins Eurovision Song Contest with 'Puppet on a String' sung by Sandie Shaw

Expo 67 World Trade Fair opens in Canada, marking the 100th anniversary of the British North America Act, 1867

May

UK applies for membership of EEC

June

Six-Day War - Israel occupies West Bank, Gaza Strip, Sinai Peninsula and the Golan Heights

Barclays Bank installs first automatic cash machine in Enfield England

Above: **WATERLOO** Bulleid Merchant Navy Pacific No 35007 *Aberdeen Commonwealth* is wreathed in steam, reversing out of Waterloo Station on 7 January 1967. *Aberdeen Commonwealth* was built in 1942 as No 21C7, renumbered 35007 in 1948 and rebuilt in 1958. In this modified form the locomotive survived in traffic until the end of Southern Region steam in July 1967.

Right: **WOKING** In order to release locomotives to work ballast trains from Meldon Quarry, the Southern Region borrowed some diesel multiple units from the Western Region that for some time replaced the previously steam hauled Waterloo - Salisbury semi-fast services during the off peak. The DMUs worked between Woking and Salisbury, with connections to and from London provided by the Portsmouth line electric trains. From 2 January 1967 most of these DMU workings were replaced by electric trains, often second class only 2EPB units, to and from Basingstoke, with diesel connections thence to Salisbury. However, on Monday 9 January 1967, in bitterly cold weather, BR Standard Class '4', No 75074 has been provided to work the 1.27 departure from Woking to Salisbury. The large green enamel station name plate survives on the end of the canopy, although British Rail corporate identity black on white signage has been installed along the station platforms.

The project to electrify the Waterloo to Bournemouth line entailed extensive civil engineering works, including the relaying of the route with continuously welded rail, together with deep ballasting and the rationalisation of track layouts at a number of locations. This work got underway in 1965 and created considerable demand for motive power to operate additional engineering and ballast trains. In March 1966 No 77014 was therefore transferred from Northwich to Guildford shed, and soon gained celebrity status as the only locomotive if its type on the region. True to the reason for its transfer, No 77014 was soon to be seen on ballast trains between

Right: **ALDERSHOT** This photograph was taken from a Waterloo to Alton electric multiple unit train on 12 January 1967 and shows BR Standard Class '4', 2-6-0 No 76053 shunting at Aldershot. The motor vehicles seen on the platform ramp in the background would now be worth a considerable sum in a line up of classic cars! No 77014 *(above)* had a special status; it was the only BR Standard 3MT 2-6-0 to be transferred to the Southern Region. Built at BR Swindon works in 1954, No 77014 was allocated to the North Eastern Region for some years before moving to Northwich (near Chester) in November 1964.

Woking and Farnham tip. It was on such a working that Ray Ruffell photographed the locomotive passing through Aldershot station on 10 January 1967 (left). But this versatile locomotive was also in demand for railtour work (see pages 13-19) and on the last day of Southern Region steam, Sunday 9 July 1967 No 77014 had the distinction of heading the final steam hauled arrival into Weymouth station the 8.50pm van train from Bournemouth. Withdrawn after arrival at Weymouth, No 77014 was subsequently sold for scrap.

On 21 January 1967 No 77014 was rostered to work the 7.15am Guildford to Wokingham freight service. The scene was recorded as the train passed the photographer at the lineside between Sandhurst and Crowthorne.

No 77014 is seen (left) after arrival at Wokingham on 21 January 1967. Carrying headcode 55 a type 3 diesel passes on a working to Blisworth, while electro-diesel No E6032 waits in the yard with a freight for Ascot via Bracknell. Shortly afterwards No 77014 returned 'light engine' tender first to Guildford; this view looks back towards Wokingham station as the level crossing gates start to re-open to road traffic.

ON TOUR

5 February 1967
The South Western Suburban
Rail Tour LCGB

On Sunday 5 February 1967, the same day that NASA launched Lunar Orbiter 3, the Locomotive Club of Great Britain organised the South Western Suburban Railtour. No less than six locomotives were used during the course of this remarkable perambulation of the suburban lines emanating from Waterloo. The scheduled and actual timings of the railtour, together with details of the locomotives used for each section, are given on the next two pages.

Left: **TWICKENHAM** Bulleid West Country Pacific No 34100 *Appledore* was in charge of the train between Shepperton and Twickenham. Having come off the Shepperton branch and passed through Strawberry Hill station, the train is seen here crossing the flyover above the line from Waterloo to Staines a short distance west of Twickenham station. At Twickenham BR Standard Class '3', 2-6-0 No 77014 was attached to the rear of the train which then proceeded westwards along the tracks beneath the flyover. *Appledore* was built in 1949, rebuilt in 1960 and withdrawn in July 1967.

Below: **WIMBLEDON PARK** A run to Chessington South was followed by a return to Wimbledon, where the train was reversed at Wimbledon Park, with BR Standard Class '4', 2-6-4 tank No 80145 then providing the motive power for the onward journey to Shepperton via Raynes Park and Kingston. This photograph was taken through the carriage window as the train approached Wimbledon Park and shows No 80145 waiting in the sidings prior to coupling to the rear of the train. BR Standard EPB and a Bulleid designed 4SUB electric multiple units can be seen in the background. The depot for electric trains at Wimbledon Park was established in 1915 when the London & South Western Railway commenced electric services between Waterloo and Wimbledon via East Putney. The LSWR also built a power station nearby at Durnsford Road which for some years supplied a large part of the Southern's electrified system, but from the 1950s onwards all power was taken from the National Grid and Durnsford Road power station was demolished in 1965.

READING The view from the footplate as BR Standard Class '4', 2-6-0 No 76058 approaches Reading General station.

Right: **HAMPTON COURT** A string of builders' temporary lights helps to illuminate the dusk as No 77014 rests by the buffer stop after arrival at Hampton Court.

Route :

Loco(s)	Route
77014	London Waterloo - (via Windsor through lines) - Clapham Junction - Point Pleasant Jn - East Putney - Wimbledon (local line) - Raynes Park - Motspur Park - Chessington South
77014	Chessington South - Wimbledon - Wimbledon Park
80145	Wimbledon Park - Wimbledon (through line) - Raynes Park (local line) - Kingston - Fulwell - Shepperton
34100	Shepperton - Fulwell - Twickenham
77014	Twickenham - Feltham - Staines
77014	Staines - Windsor & Eaton Riverside
34100	Windsor & Eaton Riverside - Staines - Staines Loop
76033	Staines Loop - Staines - Ascot - Reading General
76058	Reading General - Coley Branch Jn - Reading Central Goods
76058	Reading Central Goods - Reading General - Ascot - Virginia Water
34077	Virginia Water - Weybridge (local line) - Surbiton
77014	Surbiton - Hampton Court
34077	Hampton Court - Hampton Court Jn (local line) - Wimbledon - Clapham Junction - London Waterloo

Timings:

M.C	Location	Booked	Actual
0.00	Waterloo	08.45d	08.45
2.50	Queens Road	?	08/51
3.71	Clapham Junction	08/52	08/53
5.06	Point Pleasant Jn	08/55	08/56
05.57	East Putney	08/58	08/58
08.43	Wimbledon	09/07 (local lines)	09/06
09.76	Raynes Park	09/10	09/10
11.04	Motspur Park	09/12	09/13
15.20	Chessington South	09.21a ~ 09.35d	09.23 ~ 09.35
19.36	Motspur Park	09/45	09/43
20.44	Raynes Park	09/48	09/48
21.77	Wimbledon	09*52a ~ 09*59d	09.52 ~ 10.00

Miles	Station	Booked	Actual
22.74	Wimbledon Park	10L02a ~ 10L12d	10.04 ~ 10.14
23.71	Wimbledon	10/15	10.20
25.24	Raynes Park	10/20	10.23
26.35	New Malden	10/24	10.26
28.61	Kingston	10/29	10.31
30.26	Teddington	10/34	10.34½
31.43	Fulwell Jn	10/38	?
33.16	Hampton	10*42a ~ 10*48d	10.43½ ~ 10.45
37.42	Shepperton	10L58a ~ 11L10d	10.57 ~ 11.09
43.41	Fulwell Jn	11/21	11/20
44.55	Twickenham	11L28a ~ 11L41d	11.25 ~ 11.40½
46.68	Feltham Jn	11/48	11/48
52.37	Staines	11/57	11/57
59.06	Windsor & Eton Riverside	12L09a ~ 12L45d	12.09 ~ 12.44
65.60	Staines Loop	13L00a ~ 13L10d	12.58½ ~ 13.09
69.79	Virginia Water	13/20	13/18½
75.64	Ascot	13/30	13/28
83.33	Wokingham	13/40	13/40½
87.28	Earley	13/45	13/45½
89.19	Reading Spur	13/48	13/49
90.04	Reading General	13L50a ~ 14L02d	13.56 ~ 14.09
91.65	Southcote Jn (Coley Branch Jn)	14/08	14/12½
93.46	Reading Central Goods	14.18a ~ 14.40d	14.29 ~ 14.49
95.27	Southcote Jn (Coley Branch Jn)	14/52	14/57
97.08	Reading General	14L58a ~ 15L03d	15.08 ~ 15.11½
97.73	Reading Spur	15/06	15/15
99.64	Earley	15/11	15/20
103.59	Wokingham	15/18	15/24
111.28	Ascot	15/32	15/35
117.73	Virginia Water	15L46a ~ 16L03d	15.45 ~ 16.11
119.53	Chertsey	16/12	16/15
122.69	Weybridge	16/22	16/25
128.52	Hampton Court Jn	16/37	16/35½
129.76	Surbiton	16L39a ~ 16L50d	16.39 ~ 16.50
132.69	Hampton Court	17L00a ~ 17L35d	16.58 ~ 17.35
134.58	Hampton Court Jn	17/42	17/41
140.47	Wimbledon	17/51	17.53a ~ 17.59d
143.73	Clapham Junction	17/57	18/05
147.64	Waterloo	18.05a	18.15

Source: Your author would like to thank Gary Thornton and the team at the excellent

SIX BELLS JUNCTION

web site (www.sixbellsjunction.co.uk), in particular Terry Jackson & John Broderick who submitted the timings (Booked & Actual), for permission to reproduce the tour timing details.

Left: **READING** BR Standard Class '4', No 76058 was used for the trip down the short branch to Reading Central Goods Yard at Coley, where there was a 20 minute stop. The enthusiasts certainly took full advantage of this time to explore a part of the railway system that they would not normally be able to visit. Reading Central Goods Yard was in use from May 1908 until July 1983, and nothing remains of it in 2007, the site having been completely obliterated by realigned main roads.

Below: **SHEPPERTON** The branch to Shepperton opened in November 1864, and was electrified by the London & South Western Railway in 1916. The railtour was hauled into Shepperton Station by BR Standard Class '4', tank No 80145 *(see page 13)*, after arrival at Shepperton Bulleid West Country Pacific No 34100 *Appledore* was coupled to the other end of the train to take charge of the return journey along the branch; a 12 minute stop was allowed for this and a crowd has gathered beneath the traditional semaphore signal to watch. The South Western Suburban was the 100th railtour to be organised by the Locomotive Club of Great Britain, a fact commemorated by the headboards and disc on the front of the locomotive.

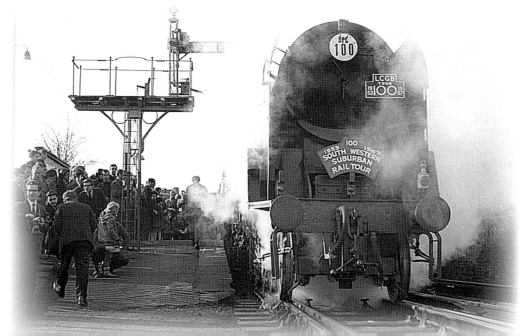

Below: **HAMPTON COURT** Class '3', 2-6-0 No 77014 had brought the special into Hampton Court at 5.00pm *(see page 15).* After arrival, Bulleid Battle of Britain Pacific No 34077 *603 Squadron* was attached to the other end of the train for the final leg of the trip back to Waterloo. *603 Squadron* was built in 1948, rebuilt in 1960 and withdrawn in March 1967. Many of the excursionists have gathered to admire the Bulleid locomotive at the head of the rake of Bulleid stock. For some reason the 4SUB unit at the platform on the right, also designed by Bulleid, and of similar vintage to *603 Squadron*, does not merit a second glance! Notice a very rare phenomenon by the ramp of this; platform a female railway enthusiast! For some reason, interest in transport seems to be an almost exclusively masculine preserve, but here we see an exception to the rule - or a very obliging girlfriend!

WINDSOR & EATON RIVERSIDE

Earlier in the day BR Standard Class '3', No 77014 had hauled the train from Twickenham to Windsor & Eton Riverside, where the train is seen (below right) after arrival at 12.09pm. The LSWR route to Windsor was opened in 1849 and the station buildings, designed by Sir William Tite, were completed in 1851. The platform illustrated here no longer exists in 2009, having been covered by a modern office development, but at least most of the station building remains, although the original ticket office is now a wine bar! The lads contemplating No 77014 are clad mostly in gaberdine raincoats; typical attire for schoolboys at that time.

1967 Happenings (2)

July
First colour television broadcasts begin on BBC 2 (full colour service commenced on BBC 2 from 2 December)
Decriminalisation of homosexuality in England
Steam traction eliminated on Southern Region of British Rail

August
Marine Broadcasting Offences Act outlaws pirate radio stations

September
RMS Queen Mary makes her final transatlantic voyage
BBC introduces Radio 1, Radio 2, Radio 3 & Radio 4

October
Abortion legalised in defined circumstances
Charles De Gaulle vetoes British entry into EEC

November
Hither Green rail crash
BBC opens first local radio station in Leicester
£ sterling devalued from $2.80 to $2.40

December
World's first heart transplant operation carried out by Christian Barnard in Cape Town, South Africa

1967
Arrivals & Departures

Births

Mark Lamarr	TV & Radio presenter	7 January
Dale Gordon	Footballer	29 January
Tamsin Greig	Actress	23 February
Jonathan Firth	Actor	6 April
Noel Gallagher	Musician	29 May
Nicole Kidman	Actress	20 June
Pamela Anderson	Actress	1 July
Tara Fitzgerald	Actress	18 September
Davina McCall	Actress	16 October
Julia Roberts	Actress	28 October
Gavin Rossdale	Musician	30 October
Letitia Dean	Actress	14 November

Deaths

Ann Sheriden	Actress	(b.1915)	21 January
Victor Gollancz	Publisher	(b.1893)	8 February
Nelson Eddy	Musician	(b.1901)	6 March
Konrad Adenauer	Chancellor of Germany	(b.1876)	19 April
John Masefield	Poet	(b.1878)	12 May
Spencer Tracy	Actor	(b.1900)	10 June
Jayne Mansfield	Actress	(b.1933)	29 June
Vivien Leigh	Actress	(b.1913)	8 July
Joe Orton	Playwright	(b.1933)	9 August
Siegfried Sassoon	Poet	(b.1886)	1 September
Sir Malcolm Sargent	Musician	(b.1895)	3 October
Woody Guthrie	Musician	(b.1912)	3 October
Clement Attlee	UK Prime Minister	(b.1883)	8 October
Sydney Barnes	Cricketer	(b.1873)	26 December
Paul Whiteman	Musician	(b.1890)	29 December

Below: **ASH** BR Standard Class '5', 4-6-0 No 73093 is watched with interest by a lad standing near the end of the platform on the right; the locomotive is running 'light engine' tender first through Ash after having worked the 7.15am Guildford to Wokingham freight service on 11 February 1967. The signal box glimpsed in the right background dates from 1964.

Right: **WEYBRIDGE** In 1967 newspapers for the provinces were normally transported by night trains from London, often being sorted en-route into bundles for subsequent distribution by wholesalers to various retail outlets. During the daytime the empty vans from the newspaper trains had to be returned to London for the following night's service. BR Standard Class '5', 4-6-0 No 76069 is passing through Weybridge with such a working on 31 March 1967. Note the 2EPB unit just visible in the bay platform on the right. This is waiting to depart for Staines via Chertsey, a route that has been worked by electric trains since 3 January 1937. The 2EPB unit we see here is one of a batch of 34 such units built at Eastleigh in 1958-9 using underframes that had been recovered from withdrawn 2NOL units. The bodywork of this batch of 2EPB units was built to the Southern Railway Bulleid design - over 10 years after nationalisation and indeed several years after the construction of a batch of 2EPB units to BR Standard design. These 34 units were the very last Bulleid designed carriages to be built, and were often to be seen working the service illustrated here and also on the Waterloo to Windsor line.

During the first six months of 1967 a number of steam specials were operated on the main line from Waterloo for railway enthusiasts and others who wanted special memories of the final period of Southern Region steam traction.

One such railtour was the Dorset Coast Express organised by the Locomotive Club of Great Britain, which ran on Sunday 7 May 1967. The principal locomotive for this tour was Bulleid West Country Pacific No 34023 *Blackmoor Vale*, seen *(far right)* after arrival at Weymouth. However the itinerary for the day was a little unusual in that it included two trips down the scenic Swanage branch. This entailed the use of additional motive power; BR Standard Class '5', No 73029 is seen *(below)*, while BR Standard Class '4', No 76026 is seen *(below right)* on the rear of the train after arrival at Swanage during the first trip down the branch. Later in the day BR Standard Class '4', No 80011 was pictured *(right)* at the same location ready to return to Corfe Castle and Wareham on the second of the two trips down the branch. The regular passenger service between Wareham and Swanage had been converted from steam to diesel operation in September 1966 using three car 'Hampshire' multiple unit sets, but fortunately railtours such as the Dorset Coast Express ensured that steam was still sometimes seen on the Swanage branch during the first half of 1967.

ON TOUR
7 May 1967
The LCGB
DORSET
COAST EXPRESS

WAREHAM BR

Standard Class '4', 2-6-4T No 80011 shunts around the Dorset Coast Express just East of Wareham station during the early afternoon of Sunday 7 May 1967 The view *(right)*, taken through a carriage door droplight, looks South on the level crossing at Wareham station. The Railway Hotel in fact is older than the railway itself; this hostelry opened in 1823 as the Country House and the name was changed to the Railway Hotel when the Southampton and Dorchester Railway opened the line through Wareham in 1847. In 2009 this building is an Indian restaurant called Monsoon. The level crossing remained as a notorious bottleneck on the A351 (the principal road access to the Isle of Purbeck) until April 1980 when a flyover was built to take traffic over the railway, although a foot crossing remains at this location.

Uniquely still surrounded by Saxon earthen walls, and boasting what in 2009 must surely be the only remaining gas lit cinema in the UK, the delightful town of Wareham is well worth a visit.

Below **WEYMOUTH:** Double headed by BR Standard Class '4', No 76026 and BR Standard Class '5', No 73029, the Dorset Coast Express awaits departure from Weymouth station on 7 May. Note the 'fire devil' beside the water column to prevent freezing in severe weather.

Inset right **WEYMOUTH:** The crew of No 76026 are ready for the stiff 1 in 50 climb to Bincombe Tunnel.

Below right **CORFE CASTLE:** Proceeding towards Swanage, the Dorset Coast Express has made a stop for photographic purposes at Corfe Castle. West Country Pacific No 34023 *Blackmoor Vale* was built in 1946, withdrawn from BR service in July 1967 and subsequently preserved. In 2009 this magnificent locomotive is based on the Bluebell Railway in East Sussex; at the time of writing the loco is out of service awaiting overhaul.

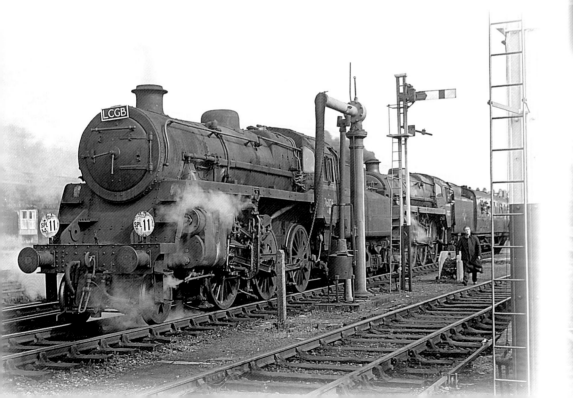

Below **WEYMOUTH:** The two BR Standard locomotives have attracted the attention of photographers as they await departure time with the Dorset Coast Express at Weymouth on 7 May.

Below centre **WEYMOUTH:** West Country Pacific No 34023 had brought the train into Weymouth, and also has attracted a number of admirers while waiting at the buffer stops. Weymouth station was originally built by the Great Western Railway, but trains from Waterloo had always enjoyed running powers between Dorchester and Weymouth, the tracks being of dual gauge until the GWR converted the line between Yeovil and Weymouth from broad to standard gauge in 1874. In 1950 the station came fully under Southern Region control and an additional island platform (out of sight to the right of this photograph) was added in 1957. This 1957 island platform forms the nucleus of the present (2009) Weymouth station, which was rebuilt to occupy a much smaller area in 1986.

Below: **SWANAGE** With part of the impressive Bell and Cronin train indicator board visible in the background, Blackmoor Vale is seen at the buffer stops in Swanage station. Subsequently closed by British Rail in January 1972, the Swanage branch has been reopened between Swanage and Norden (near Corfe Castle) by preservationists and a visit is highly recommended, but sadly the Bell and Cronin indicator board is no more, having been declared a surplus anachronism by British Rail and destroyed.

WOKING Quite a variety of rolling stock has been provided for this morning commuter train from Salisbury to Waterloo, seen *(below left)* approaching Woking on 12 May 1967. The two carriages nearest to the locomotive, a popular part of the train at this time of day with those who want to make a quick dash for the Underground (or office) on arrival in London, consist of BR Standard Mark I non-corridor compartment carriages. This certainly provided the highest possible seating capacity, but such accommodation was hardly ideal for an end-to-end journey of over 83 miles. The rest of the train is an assortment of Bulleid and BR Standard Mark I corridor carriages. Providing the motive power is Bulleid Battle of Britain Pacific No 34052 *Lord Dowding*, built in 1946, rebuilt in 1958 and subsequently withdrawn from service at Salisbury shed on 9 July 1967.

EASTLEIGH By May 1967 some electric trains were running in steam timings on the Waterloo to Bournemouth line, the final section of conductor rail (that between Lymington Junction and Bournemouth) having been energised in March of that year. Deliveries of the high powered 4REP electric multiple units that were to form the backbone of the updated service were running late however, and electric multiple units were borrowed from elsewhere on the Southern Region to keep services running during the summer of 1967. It was not unusual to see trains made up of 2HAP multiple units dating from the late 1950s working on stopping services at this time, and it is from such a train that this interesting photograph *(below right)* was taken on 9 May 1967. A REP/TC formation, a combination that was to become very familiar for the next 20 years, approaches on a down service to Bournemouth, while a BR Standard Class '4', 4-6-0 on a van train waits at the colour light signal. In the yard Birmingham RCW Type 3 diesel No D6523 is at the head of a train of oil tank wagons. Known also as 'Cromptons', the D65XX locomotives were to remain an everyday sight for many more years, especially as 19 of the class were fitted for push-pull working and used in conjunction with 4TC trailer units on passenger services west of Bournemouth from 1967 until electrification was finally extended from Branksome to Weymouth in 1988.

1967 TV Favourites; a selection

The Forsyte Saga

John Galsworthy's novels about a well-to-do London family were made into a twenty six part serial that commenced in January 1967 on BBC 2. Starring such famous actors as Kenneth Moore, Eric Porter and Susan Hampshire, this epic was extremely popular and was repeated in 1968 on BBC 1.

The Prisoner

Filmed in the unique Italianate Welsh village of Portmeirion, this bizarre cult serial was written by and starred Patrick McGoohan.

Dee Time

A popular tea-time chat show, with disc jockey Simon Dee.

The Golden Shot

The idea for this game show originated in Switzerland, and it was brought to British television screens in 1967 by ATV, with Jackie Rae as the first host.

News at Ten

ITN took a major step forward in July when the chimes of Big Ben interspersed by the headlines of the day introduced the first edition of the news programme that fast became a national institution.

Face the Music

This enjoyable test of musical knowledge was hosted by Joseph Cooper.

Never Mind the Quality, Feel the Width

This gentle comedy was set in a tailor's shop and starred John Bluthal and Joe Lynch.

Mickey Dunne

In the words of the catchy signature tune 'Mickey Dunne - he's a friend to anyone; in a tricky spot it's as like as not that he's the one who'll be holding the baby'. Dinsdale Landen played the eponymous hero who would chase anything young in a (mini) skirt, in this comedy drama series that was screened on BBC 1 in the spring/summer of 1967.

On 27 May 1967 the rebuilt Bulleid
Light Pacific on a down train leaving
Waterloo is 'framed' between the
locomotives of two incoming services.

THE KENNY BELLE:

These photographs record a service, unadvertised in 1967, that was provided during morning and afternoon peak periods between Clapham Junction and Kensington Olympia, mostly for the use of Post Office staff. The two views on the left show BR Standard Class '3', 2-6-2 tank locomotive No 82019 on 30 May and 31 May 1967 at Kensington Olympia, waiting to depart with the evening train to Clapham Junction; the photograph below shows the 'Kenny Belle' (as the service was affectionately known) after arrival at Clapham Junction.

Ivatt Class '2' 2-6-2 tank locomotives also took turns on the 'Kenny Belle', as exemplified by No 41319 nearing Clapham Junction on 6 July 1967 *(right)*. Seen from the train *(lower right)* on the approach to the main line at Clapham Junction, the motive power on 30 June 1967 was Ivatt 2-6-2T No 41312; on Saturday 2 April 1967 this locomotive had worked the last steam hauled service train on the Brockenhurst to Lymington branch.

In 2009 there is an advertised regular service of electric trains from Clapham Junction to Kensington Olympia and Willesden Junction/ Watford Junction.

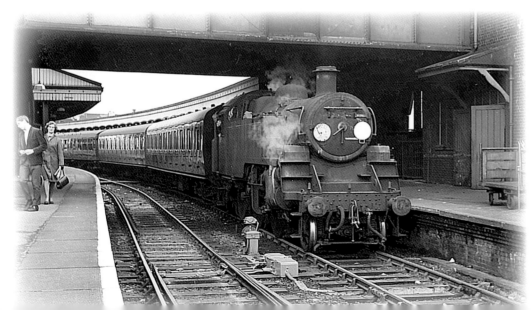

KENSINGTON
(OLYMPIA)

KENSINGTON OLYMPIA Although
the 'Kenny Belle' trains were unadvertised in
1967, by the closing weeks of steam operation
they were the focus of considerable attention
from enthusiasts. In the main photograph
Ivatt 2-6-2 tank locomotive No 41312 is being
coupled up at Kensington Olympia ready to
return to Clapham Junction with the afternoon
service; Driver Walker of Nine Elms and his
fireman (inset) are clearly enjoying themselves.

41312

The last few days...

EASTLEIGH After the Second World War the Southern Railway had purchased 14 0-6-0 shunting locomotive from the United States Transportation Corps; these had been built at the Vulcan Iron Works of Wilkes-Barre, Pennsylvania, USA, to a very basic design and had been intended as a possible back up for an allied invasion of Europe during the hostilities. Following purchase by the Southern Railway, the USA tanks were put to work in Southampton Docks, where they remained until they were largely displaced by diesel shunters in 1962. These versatile little locomotives were then cascaded to a number of locations around the Southern Region, including Lancing Carriage Works, Ashford and, as photographed here on 4 June 1967, Eastleigh. Nine of these locomotives survived into 1967, with seven remaining in service until the final day of steam working, Sunday 9 July. In 2007 preserved examples can be seen on the Bluebell Railway, the Kent & East Sussex Railway and the Keighley & Worth Valley Railway.

As 10 July, the first day to be completely devoid of steam traction on the Southern Region, drew closer, graffiti messages like the one seen at Waterloo in the photograph on the right became commonplace - a sad confirmation of what we all knew to be true ....

The Waterloo to Weymouth line was host to a distinguished visitor on 4 June 1967 when former LNER A4 Pacific No 4498 *Sir Nigel Gresley* worked a railtour. Built at Doncaster in 1937, this locomotive held the post war speed record for a steam locomotive, reaching 112mph on 23 May 1959. Withdrawn from British Rail service as No 60007 in February 1966, *Sir Nigel Gresley* was purchased by the A4 Locomotive Society and subsequently overhauled at Crewe, emerging in the spring of 1967 once again carrying the original LNER number 4498. This railtour enabled the famous locomotive to show its paces on the Waterloo to Weymouth line. Driver Jim Robinson of Nine Elms shed is seen (*below left*) awaiting departure from Southampton Central station, and the train also made a photographic stop at Wareham (*below*). On arrival at Weymouth (*above right*) No 4498 has attracted a crowd of admirers; the train terminated at the island platform that was added to Weymouth station in 1957, and which in 2009 forms the nucleus of the rebuilt (and much reduced) terminus at Weymouth.

No 4498 resides in preservation on the North Yorkshire Moors Railway in 2009.

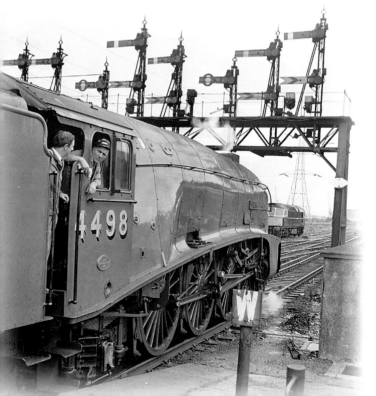

1967 Happenings (3)

The new sound of Radio 1

It was on Saturday 30 September 1967 that the BBC replaced the familiar Light Programme, Third Programme and Home Service with radio by numbers – Radios 1, 2 3 and 4, which still broadcast in 2009 albeit on different frequencies to those used in 1967.

A new departure for the BBC, Radio 1 was designed as a pop music station and intended to woo the audience of young people who had latterly listened to the recently outlawed 'pirate' stations. Originally Radio 1 was allocated one frequency only, 247 metres medium wave, with no FM coverage. Radio 2 continued to use the high power transmitter at Droitwich previously used by the Light Programme, which gave satisfactory reception on 1500 metres long wave over most of the UK, plus the station enjoyed FM transmissions giving a high quality of sound. Prior to 30 September 1967, 247 metres Medium Wave had been used by 16 low power relay transmitters for the Light Programme; initially these continued as the sole transmitters of Radio 1. Whilst London and the Home Counties had reasonable reception from Brookmans Park and much of the North of England had a strong signal from Moorside Edge, the most powerful Radio 1 transmitter initially was at Washford in Somerset. This meant that many areas of the UK could not get satisfactory reception on Radio 1 when the station was first introduced – a problem that became more noticeable during the hours of darkness when interference from other stations increased markedly.

Steps were later taken to improve the situation by increasing the power of some transmitters and providing a few local relays (for example at Bournemouth on 202 metres) but it took 21 years for Radio 1 to gain an all day presence on FM!

EASTLEIGH A sad scene at Eastleigh *(main photograph below)* on Friday 7 July 1967. A group of condemned steam locomotives, with Bulleid West Country Pacific No 34040 *Crewkerne* nearest the camera, wait their turn to be towed away to the scrapyard. In contrast the Brush and Birmingham RCW diesel and the electro-diesel seen towards the right of the photograph await their next turn of duty.

The signal arm seen on the corner of the large water tank behind the steam locomotives was used to test drivers' eyesight, and had no role in the regulation of train movements.

NINE ELMS By 1967 many of the pilot and empty stock duties at Nine Elms and Waterloo had been taken over by Ivatt class '2' tank locomotives, as exemplified by this view of No 41298 *(right)* with cheerful staff. In reality, however, the scene at Nine Elms on 7 July 1967 *(far right)* showed little to be cheerful about. Photographed from a down express on the main line, very little activity can be seen in this once busy location. The massive

locomotive coaling plant was built in 1923. Note the coal wagons in the siding to the left of the plant; the loaded wagons were hoisted up to the top of the coal stage where they were tipped upside down to empty the coal into the hopper below. Locomotive tenders were filled by gravity from this hopper. To the right of the coal stage were the foreman's and timekeepers' offices and the 'new' shed which dated from 1910.

The end is nigh...

Left: **GUILDFORD**
On Thursday 6 July 1967 BR Standard class '3', No 77014 and Bulleid Battle of Britain Pacific No 34060 *25 Squadron* stand over the ash pits by Guildford coal stage. Bulleid West Country Pacific No 34018 *Axminster* can be seen in the background.

Above: **SOUTHAMPTON** On the same day BR Standard class '4', No 76066 was running 'light engine' near Southampton while Bulleid Battle of Britain Pacific No 34087 *145 Squadron* was photographed approaching Southampton Central station with the 11.25 Weymouth to Waterloo service. Note the mixed formation of the train - quite a contrast the neat sets of Bulleid or BR Standard Mark 1 carriages that had been usual until a few years previously.

Right: **EASTLEIGH** BR Standard Class '4', 2-6-4 tank locomotive No 80016 was also active on 6 July, and is seen on freight duties in Eastleigh yard in this photograph taken from a passing train.

Last fleeting glimpses...

WEYBRIDGE: The very last steam hauled service train to Waterloo; Merchant Navy Class No 35030 *Elder Dempster Lines* runs through Weybridge at 70mph with the 2.07pm from Weymouth on Sunday 9 July.

The very last day

1967
No 1 Records

January
   Green Green Grass of Home   Tom Jones
   I'm a Believer   Monkees
February
   This is my Song   Petula Clark
March
   Release Me   Englebert Humperdink
April
   Somethin' Stupid   Frank Sinatra &
   Nancy Sinatra
   Puppet on a String   Sandie Shaw
May
   Silence is Golden   Tremeloes
June
   A Whiter Shade of Pale   Procul Harum
July
   All You Need is Love   Beatles
August
   San Francisco   Scott Mckenzie
September
   The Last Waltz   Englebert Humperdink
October
   Massachusetts   Bee Gees
November
   Baby, Now That I've Found You Foundations
   Let The Heartache Begin Long John Baldry
December
   Hello Goodbye   Beatles

The last journey...

BASINGSTOKE: Type 3 diesel No D6542 approaches Basingstoke station from the east on Sunday 23 July hauling three redundant steam locomotives *(see also next page)*. Note the new and old signal boxes in the background.

BASINGSTOKE: On the morning of Monday 10 July 1967 we awoke to the realisation that steam haulage on the Southern Region was no more. Indeed British Rail seemed keen to remove any equipment from the steam era as quickly as possible; such items as water columns disappeared from station platforms with almost indecent haste. Ironically, but perhaps inevitably, the replacement electric services between Waterloo and Bournemouth took several months to settle down and become reliable, and with a number of the new 4REP multiple units sometimes being unavailable for service it is suspected that the traffic department would on occasion have welcomed the ability to press a Merchant Navy Class loco and a rake of Bulleid carriages into use!

Alas, it was not to be, although during the first few weeks of the electric era steam locomotives were to be seen on the move along the main line in altogether sadder circumstances. Many withdrawn locomotives were taken to Weymouth or Salisbury, where some remained in storage until early 1968 before being transferred to various scrap yards.

On Sunday 23 July, exactly a fortnight after the last day of Southern Region steam, D6542 hauls BR Standard Class '4', 2-6-4T No 80151, BR Standard Class '4MT' No 76058 and BR Standard Class '4', 2-6-4T No 80141 west through Basingstoke on their way to Salisbury for storage and eventual disposal.

20T
B952532

Acknowledgements

It would not have been possible to produce this book without the use of the wonderful collection of photographs taken by the late Ray Ruffell; all of the illustrations in this volume started in his camera.

Ray was a railwayman by profession, but his interest in transport went far beyond his day to day work. In his off duty time Ray travelled widely throughout the British Isles, and in doing so created an extensive photographic recode of the railway system at a time when great changes were underway. Many scenes that were everyday and commonplace when Ray photographed them have now been swept away for ever and the memories he has captured on film, precious at the time, are now beyond price. It is pleasing to record that this huge collection of photographs has been kept complete and is now in the safe keeping of The NOSTALGIA Collection forming an important part of their photographic archives.

I would like to say a sincere thank you to the team at The NOSTALGIA Collection for inviting me to write this book, which I hope will be a worthy member of the Railways and Recollections series. The cheerful and willing help I have received from Peter Townsend, Will Adams, Mick Sanders and David Walshaw has been warmly appreciated and I feel deeply honoured to work with such kind people. I would also like to record my thanks to Andrew Wickham, Operations Director and Alex Carter, Managing Director of the Wilts & Dorset Bus Company for their help and encouragement with this project.

And so we end our nostalgic look back at 1967 with a relic of the past that Ray Ruffell captured on film at Guildford Locomotive Depot on 26 November. Water Tender D53002, lettered Return to Hove' was marshalled into a tunnel repair train when photographed, and evidence of previous Southern Railway ownership was still discernable over 19 years after the demise of that Company!

I hope you have enjoyed this look back at 1967 and that you will want to sample more years in the Railways and Recollections series.

Chris Harris